TULSA CITY-COUNTY LIBRARY

S0-AAH-295

ouch! hello! alas! hi! hey! um! wow! ah! meow! hmm! rats! eh! you well! oh, dear!

THE MAGIC OF LANGUAGE

Interjections

yo! hey! wow! hi! yippee! hurray!

By Ann Heinrichs

THE CHILD'S WORLD®
CHANHASSEN, MINNESOTA

Published in the United States of America by The Child's World®
PO Box 326, Chanhassen, MN 55317-0326
800-599-READ
www.childsworld.com

Content Adviser:
Kathy Rzany, M.A.,
Adjunct Professor,
School of Education,
Dominican University,
River Forest, Illinois

Photo Credits: Cover photograph: Punchstock/Digital Vision Interior photographs:
Corbis: 7 (James W. Porter), 13 (Lucidio Studio Inc.), 24 (Images.com), 29 (Robert
Dowling); David Young-Wolff/PhotoEdit/Picture Quest: 27; Getty Images: 16 (The
Image Bank/Andre Gallant), 22 (Taxi/Andreas Kuehn); Getty Images/PhotoDisc: 10
(Ryan McVay), 15; Getty Images/Stone: 5 (Dave Nagel), 18 (Ron Alston); Magnum
Photos/Steve McCurry: 25; Punchstock/Digital Vision: 20.

The Child's World®: Mary Berendes, Publishing Director

Editorial Directions, Inc.: E. Russell Primm, Editorial Director; Pam Rosenberg,
Project Editor; Melissa McDaniel, Line Editor; Katie Marsico, Assistant Editor;
Matt Messbarger, Editorial Assistant; Susan Hindman, Copyeditor; Susan Ashley and
Sarah E. De Capua, Proofreaders; Chris Simms and Olivia Nellums, Fact Checkers;
Timothy Griffin/IndexServ, Indexer; Cian Loughlin O'Day and Dawn Friedman,
Photo Researchers; Linda S. Koutris, Photo Selector

The Design Lab: Kathleen Petelinsek, Design and Page Production;
Kari Thornborough, Page Production Assistant

Copyright © 2004 by The Child's World®
All rights reserved. No part of this book may be reproduced or utilized in
any form or by any means without written permission from the publisher.

Library of Congress Cataloging-in-Publication Data
Heinrichs, Ann.
  Interjections / by Ann Heinrichs.
      v. cm. — (The magic of language)
Includes index.
Contents: What is an interjection?—Words that stand alone—Wait! stop! it's a verb!—
Happy interjections—Not-so-happy interjections—Ways to fill up space—Interjections
with no words—Bang! zap! pow!—Interjections around the world—Do animals have
interjections?
  ISBN 1-59296-072-3 (lib. bdg. : alk. paper)
  1. English language—Interjections—Juvenile literature. [1. English language—
Interjections.] I. Title.
  PE1355.H446 2004
  425—dc22   2003021405

TABLE OF CONTENTS

J 428.2 H364i 2004
Heinrichs, Ann.
Interjections

CHAPTER ONE

What Is an Interjection?

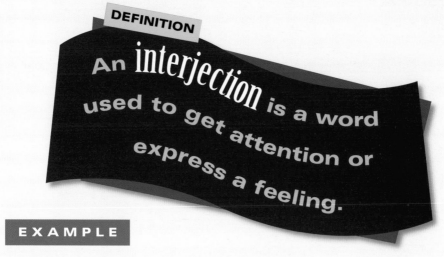

DEFINITION

An **interjection** is a word used to get attention or express a feeling.

EXAMPLE

Wow! Yahoo! Ouch! Yuk! Yum!

Guess what all these words are? They're interjections! Can you imagine life without them? You'd have lots of trouble saying how you feel. Interjections are words you use to get attention or express feelings.

Some interjections express happiness, sadness, or surprise.

EXAMPLE

Yippee! It's party time!
Alas, the library is closed today.
Eek! There's a mouse under my chair!

All these kids are yelling a big, loud interjection. What do you suppose that interjection is?

Some interjections are cheers.

EXAMPLE

Hurray! We finally won after all these years!
Bravo! You did a great job!

Some interjections are greetings or good-byes.

EXAMPLE

Hi, Sarah. How's your hamster?
So long, Bart.

And some interjections just sort of fill up space!

EXAMPLE

We only have, **um,** 50 videos.
Well, make sure you get some more.

DID YOU KNOW?

The word *interjection* comes from two Latin words—*inter* ("between") and *jactus* ("thrown"). So an interjection is a word "thrown between" other words.

Some experts say interjections are the earliest form of human speech. Imagine cavemen or prehistoric hunters. They might have spoken to each other in grunts and shouts. They might have said things that meant **Hey!** or **Whoopee!** or **Wow!**

Our communication has developed much more since then, but

we still need lots of interjections. Let's check it out!

Early hunters probably used interjections to communicate with one another about hunting.

CHAPTER TWO

WORDS THAT STAND ALONE

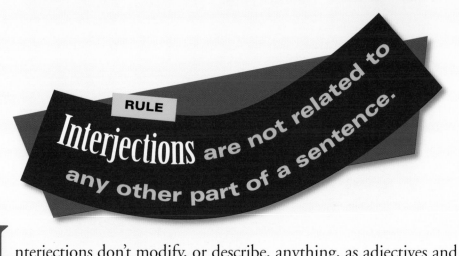

RULE

Interjections are not related to any other part of a sentence.

I nterjections don't modify, or describe, anything, as adjectives and adverbs do. They don't name anything, as nouns and pronouns do. They're not action words, as verbs are. And they don't join words together, as prepositions and conjunctions do. They just stand alone.

When speaking, it's easy to make an interjection stand alone. Often you just say the interjection and stop. Sometimes you naturally make a little pause in your voice before going on.

What about when you're writing interjections? You still need to make the interjection stand alone. You need to show what your voice would be doing if you were speaking. You do that with

punctuation marks.

RULE

Strong interjections are followed by an exclama-tion point. Mild interjections are set off by commas.

You can often spot an interjection. It's followed by an exclamation

point (!). The exclamation point comes after strong interjections—

those that express strong feelings. Maybe you're excited. Maybe you're

even yelling!

EXAMPLE

Oops! My monkey jumped off its perch.
Hey! Get that monkey off my head!
Yoo-hoo! Come back here, Frisky.

There are no bananas for this little fellow today. If he could talk,
*would he use the strong interjection **Darn!** or the mild interjection **Gee?***

Some interjections are calmer and quieter. They're called mild

interjections. To make mild interjections stand alone, use commas (,).

E X A M P L E

Say, do you have any bananas for my monkey?

No, we have no bananas today.

Well, when will you have bananas?

Gee, I really don't know.

CHAPTER THREE

WAIT! STOP! IT'S A VERB!

EXAMPLE

Stop! Look! Help! Wait! Stay!

All these words have exclamation points. They're spoken with strong feelings, and they stand alone. They're words you might call out or even yell at the top of your voice. But watch out! They're not interjections. They're really verbs.

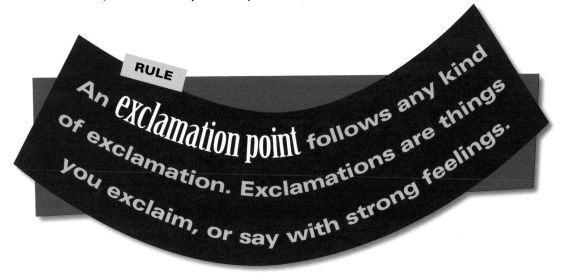

RULE

An exclamation point follows any kind of exclamation. Exclamations are things you exclaim, or say with strong feelings.

Exclamation points are good clues for finding interjections.

However, not every exclamation point means you have an interjection. Exclamation points follow any kind of exclamation. Exclamations are things you exclaim, or call out with strong feelings such as excitement or surprise.

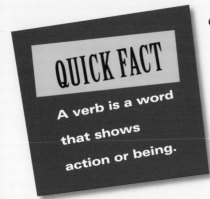

QUICK FACT

A verb is a word that shows action or being.

Each word in the example is an action word. **Stop** is an action. So are **look, help, wait,** and **stay.** These words all describe things to do or ways to be. Therefore, they are verbs.

DEFINITION

A sentence is a group of words that expresses a complete thought and ends with a period or exclamation point. Every sentence has a subject and a verb.

Wait! There's more. **Stop!** and **Look!** and the other examples are also complete sentences. All sentences have a subject and a verb. We know where the verb is. But where is the subject?

The subject is **you.** We don't see or say the word **you.**

*She's saying **Stop!** There's no doubt about it—she means **You stop!***

However, **you** is understood when commands are given. **Stop!** and

Look! are commands. If someone says **Stop!** to you, you know it

means **You stop!**

CHAPTER FOUR

Happy Interjections

Surprise, delight, and other happy feelings are perfect reasons to use interjections. Suppose you just found out you won 100 free pizzas. Which of these interjections would you use?

EXAMPLE

> **Wow! Gosh! Golly! Gee whiz! Yeow! Yowie! My goodness! Oh boy!**

When your friends found out about the pizzas, they might break into cheers:

EXAMPLE

> **Hurray! Yay! Yahoo! Yippee! Whoopee! Right on!**

When you eat the pizzas, your interjections might be **Yum!** or **Yummy!** or **Mmm!**

If you're trying to get someone's attention, you say **Hey!** or maybe **Yoo-hoo!** Greetings and good-byes have interjections,

too—**hi, hello,**

good-bye,

bye, and

so long.

Ha! can

mean "Oh boy!"

or "See there!" or

"I don't believe

that." If you came up with a great

idea, you'd say **Aha!** But if you're

laughing, you say **Ha-ha!**

And don't forget Santa!

EXAMPLE

Merry Christmas!
Ho ho ho!

What interjection do you think he is yelling?

DID YOU KNOW?

In a way, **good-bye** is a whole sentence. It's a short form of the old English farewell, "God be with you."

CHAPTER FIVE

NOT-SO-HAPPY
INTERJECTIONS

Many interjections are things you say when you're not so

happy. Maybe you're shocked or disappointed. Maybe you're

annoyed. Maybe you're just plain sad. Whatever your feelings are,

there's an interjection to help you express them.

*This little boy is feeling sad. He might be thinking of interjections such as **Oh dear.***

Suppose you did your homework, but the dog ate it. Which of these interjections would you use?

E X A M P L E

Nuts! Darn! Shoot!
Oh dear! Alas!

If you're scared, displeased, or just fed up, there are plenty of interjections for you!

E X A M P L E

Eek! I saw a snake in the grass.
Yikes! There's a whole nest of ants!
Yuk! Some broccoli just landed in my ice cream!
Ouch! That mosquito bit my leg!
Uh-oh! Sparky turned the garbage can over again.
Good grief! He's been running in circles for an hour.

If something is annoying you, you have a choice of interjections.

Scram! means "Go away!" To make a flying insect go away, you wave your hands in the air and say **Shoo!** One interjection is just for cats—**Scat!**

Uh-oh! His dog just turned the garbage can over. Darn! He has to clean it up.

What if someone says your kitty is afraid of mice? You might say

Not! But if you say "No way!" they might say **Way!**

Suppose there was a big announcement on the news: "Scientists

have discovered that chickens lay eggs."

There's only one interjection for this situation: **Duh!**

CHAPTER SIX

WAYS TO FILL UP SPACE

Some interjections seem to have no purpose. They just seem to fill up space. But they can be very helpful in conversation. For example, interjections can "get you going" when you start to say something.

EXAMPLE

Gee, I'm getting really tired.
So, you think you've had enough?
Oh, I thought it was time to go.
Well, try not to be late next time.
Say, where did you put that lizard?
Boy, that was a loud noise.

Sometimes when you're talking, you need to stop and think a second. Interjections fill that gap while you're thinking.

EXAMPLE

We should be done by, **uh,** three o'clock.
I wonder where Tigger is. **Hmm.** Maybe he's
    on the roof.
The last time I saw him was, **um,** Thursday.

CHAPTER SEVEN

INTERJECTIONS WITH NO WORDS

Some interjections are just sounds. Some of them seem to explode right out of your mouth! These sounds are not

words. Many of the sounds don't even exist in regular spoken English. So how can they be written down? We use certain groups of letters to stand for mouth and throat sounds.

Some interjections are just sounds that seem to explode right out of your mouth.

Did you ever clear your throat to get someone's attention? That throat-clearing sound is spelled **Ahem!** What do you say when you want someone to be quiet? You blow air past your tongue to say **Sh!** Did you ever hear a joke and start giggling? That giggling sound is spelled **hee-hee.**

Tsk-tsk stands for a clicking sound. It's made by clicking the tip of your tongue against the back of your teeth. It means "That's too bad" or "Shame on you!"

DID YOU KNOW?

The clicking sound is a regular part of speech in some African languages. They're sometimes called click languages. Speakers of these languages include the Zulu, Xhosa, San, and Khoikhoi people of southern Africa.

EXAMPLE

Tsk-tsk! That's a terrible bruise.
Tsk-tsk! You've spilled paint all over the floor.

Suppose you want to say, "Hey—over here!" very quietly. You use your lips and tongue to say **Pss!** or **Psst!** What if you narrowly

Ugh! is an interjection you use when something tastes or smells bad.

escape a disaster? You blow air through your lips to say **Whew!**

Another great interjection is **Ugh!** It's a grunt or groan way in the

back of your mouth, near your throat.

EXAMPLE

> **Psst!** I'm under the bed.
> **Whew!** That weasel almost bit my leg.
> **Ugh!** This baloney sandwich is moldy!

CHAPTER EIGHT

BANG! ZAP! POW!

Comics and cartoons are full of great interjections. Some are real words, but others just stand for sounds. They all add energy and excitement to the action. They help you hear what's happening, besides seeing it.

Zoom! and **Whoosh!** are the sounds of things flying through the air. When something lands on a hard surface, it might go **Wham!** or **Whap!** If it's wet, it goes **Splat!** Explosions might go **Boom!** or **Ka-boom!** or **Ka-blooey!**

Lots of human sounds show up in comics, too. Pirates and sailors seem to love saying **Argh!** It's more like a growl than a word. When people bump into things, they go **Oof!** or **Unh!**

Zzzzz stands for the sound of snoring. Have you ever heard

*Can you tell what's happening when you see this comic-book interjection? The interjection **Bam!** helps you hear what's happening, too.*

someone say they're going to "catch some z's"? It means they're going

to get some sleep!

Can you think of any other comic or cartoon interjections? Do

you have some favorites?

CHAPTER NINE

INTERJECTIONS AROUND THE WORLD

No matter where in the world you live, you need interjections.

It's fun to learn about interjections in other languages. Take a look at these examples. You'll see that many foreign-language interjections are very similar to English interjections.

DID YOU KNOW?

In Spanish, interjections and other exclamations get special punctuation marks. An upside-down exclamation point (¡) comes at the beginning, and a regular exclamation point comes at the end.

This Tibetan boy uses interjections just like you do.

SPANISH	PRONUNCIATION	MEANING
¡He! or ¡Eh!	eh	Hey!
¡Ay!	eye	Alas!
¡Oh!	oh	Oh!
¡Olé!	oh-LAY	Bravo!

FRENCH		
Zut!	zoot	Shoot! or Darn!
Hé!	eh	Hey! or Well!
Aïe!	eye	Ouch! or Oh dear!
Ouf!	oof	Whew!

GERMAN		
He! or Hei!	heh or hi	Hey!
Au!	ow	Oh! or Ouch!
Ach!	ahk	Alas!

In the United States, some regions and culture groups have their own interjections. In some places, **eh** is used in asking questions.

Yo is an all-purpose exclamation. It often means **hi** or **hey.**

EXAMPLE

Tired of practicing, **eh?**
Yo, Jesse. What's up?

Are there any special interjections in the area where you live?

Kids around the world use lots of interjections when they're playing. They need to express excitement, joy, disappointment, and plenty of other feelings.

CHAPTER TEN

DO ANIMALS HAVE INTERJECTIONS?

Animals can't speak in words. They can only make sounds. Like humans, they express surprise, joy, sadness, and many other feelings. So you might say they "speak" in interjections!

People have figured out ways to spell animal sounds. Some are

bow-wow, meow, quack, honk, moo, oink,

cluck-cluck, cock-

a-doodle-doo, grr,

and **hee-haw.** Can you

think of any others?

How can you tell

what an animal means?

Often you can't tell. But if

DID YOU KNOW?

BARKING AROUND THE WORLD

Other languages have their own ways of spelling animal sounds. In Japan, a barking dog says wan, wan! ("wahn, wahn"). In Ghana, it says wahu, wahu! ("WAH-hoo, WAH-hoo"). In Germany, it's wau, wau! ("wow, wow"). In Turkey, it's hav, hav! ("how, how").

you know the animal well, you might be able to figure it out. **Bow-wow!** could mean, "I'm happy to see you!" **Meow!** could mean, "I don't like that new cat food!"

Do you have a pet? Or do you know another animal well? Can you tell what some of its sounds mean?

Quack! *What is this duck trying to say? "I'm hungry"?*
"The lights are too bright"? "My toes are sticking to the floor"?

How to Learn More

At the Library

Collins, S. Harold, and Kathy Kifer (illustrator). *Prepositions, Conjunctions, and Interjections.* Eugene, Ore.: Garlic Press, 1992.

Heller, Ruth. *Fantastic! Wow! and Unreal!: A Book about Interjections and Conjunctions.* New York: Grosset & Dunlap, 1998.

Terban, Marvin, and Peter Spacek (illustrator). *Checking Your Grammar.* New York: Scholastic, 1994.

On the Web

Visit our home page for lots of links about grammar:

http://www.childsworld.com/links.html

NOTE TO PARENTS, TEACHERS AND LIBRARIANS: We routinely check our Web links to make sure they're safe, active sites—so encourage your readers to check them out!

Through the Mail or by Phone

To find a Grammar Hotline near you, contact:

THE GRAMMAR HOTLINE DIRECTORY
Tidewater Community College Writing Center
1700 College Crescent
Virginia Beach, VA 23453
Telephone: (757) 822-7170
http://www.tcc.edu/students/resources/writcent/GH/hotlino1/htm

To learn more about grammar, visit the Grammar Lady online or call her toll free hotline:

THE GRAMMAR LADY
Telephone: (800) 279-9708
www.grammarlady.com

Fun with Interjections

1. Which animal makes each of these sounds?

     a. quack

     b. moo

     c. hee-haw

     d. honk

     e. cock-a-doodle-doo

2. What are these interjections used for?

     a. boom!

     b. zzzzz!

     c. ahem!

     d. ouch!

     e. psst!

See page 32 for the answers. Don't peek!

Index

Answers

Answers to Fun with Interjections

Question 1 answers:

a. duck

b. cow

c. donkey

d. goose

e. rooster

Question 2 answers:

a. an explosion

b. snoring

c. clearing the throat

d. pain

e. getting someone's attention

About the Author

Ann Heinrichs was lucky. Every year from grade three through grade eight, she had a big, fat grammar text-book and a grammar workbook. She feels that this prepared her for life. She is now the author of more than 100 books for children and young adults. She has also enjoyed successful careers as a children's book editor and an advertising copywriter. Ann grew up in Fort Smith, Arkansas, and lives in Chicago, Illinois.